D0099510

~ Gina ~
Hope you learn lots
of new tricks.

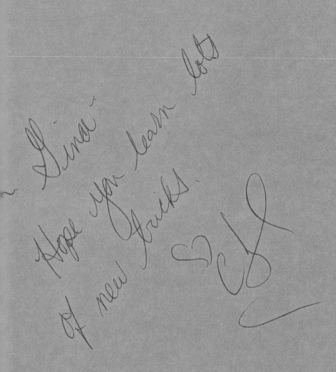

The Girls' Guide to Spells

The Girls' Guide to

Spells

Making magic happen in your life

ANTONIA BEATTIE
and
AMARGI WOLF

BARNES
&NOBLE
BOOKS
NEW YORK

Contents

INTRODUCTION: THE POWER OF SPELLS 6

WHAT YOU NEED TO KNOW ABOUT SPELLS 8

Abracadabra: Spells and how they work ★ Using your intuition
★ Making your own magic wand

USING THE POWER OF MOTHER NATURE 14

Tapping into nature's energies ★ Spells and the elements ★ Moon magic

MAKING MAGIC HAPPEN IN YOUR LIFE 20

Connecting with the Earth ★ You can make a difference: Learning to focus
★ Finding your magical name ★ Finding an animal helper ★ Finding and using
a pendulum friend ★ Your special space: Ideas for decorating your room

SPELLS AND YOU 30

Putting your own spells together step-by-step ★ Choosing the right day
★ Choosing the best season ★ Starting your own spell diary

USING CANDLES IN SPELLS 38

Choosing and preparing the right candle ★ A candle spell for attracting
good fortune ★ A candle spell for feeling good about yourself

SPELLS AT HOME 42

Doing spells for friends and family ★ Finding new friends ★ Friends in magic: Things to do together ★ Spells for a harmonious home life

SPELLS FOR SUCCESS 50

Starting a new school or job
★ A special study spell ★ Passing exams
★ Making a powerful good luck charm

SPELLS FOR PROTECTING YOURSELF 58

Giving yourself permission to feel strong ★ An invisibility spell
★ Dealing with difficult teachers and friends ★ Coping better without curses

SPELLS FOR YOUR LOVE LIFE 66

Stone casting to find out if someone loves you
★ A clarity spell to ensure you choose right ★ Getting rid of your jealousy
★ Preparing your energies for that big date
★ Attracting a new love into your life ★ Finding your true love
★ Are you compatible?

GLOSSARY 79

Introduction: The Power of Spells

Have you ever wished for something good to happen in your life? If you have, you have started doing a spell. With a spell, the first stage is to wish for something; the next is to do something about your wish. This book will show you that you have the power within yourself to reach the second stage — to make things happen in your life. It will show how you can use spells to exercise this power, and have a lot of fun doing so.

It is important to start the first stage of your spell by working out what you really want. You may want something specific, like a new friend, a boyfriend, more money or a new car, or to be thinner or have a wonderful new wardrobe of clothes. Or you may just want to be happy, and loved for who you are. You will need to realize that specific things may not bring the happiness you want. For example, getting more money will not in itself make you happier, nor will being thinner necessarily help you find your true love.

However, no matter what you want, you can use spells in wonderful, powerful ways. By doing a spell, you will not only have a chance of getting what you want, you will also have the pleasure of tapping into the vast powers of Nature. Spells will help you become more aware of the movement of the moon, the seasons of the year, the powers of the plants, stones and animals, and the other naturally occurring energies of the Earth. This will give you an enormous sense of strength. Learning how to find, raise and direct the energies of Nature will allow you to make use of this tremendous source of power — for the greatest good, for yourself, for your family and for your friends.

The spells in this book are all designed to help you gain the things you want in your life without falling into some of the usual traps with magic. They all have a positive focus, unlike spells that bind a person to you or stop them getting on with their own lives. These are particularly bad spells. Do not use them. Curses and other negative spells have the uncomfortable habit of recoiling on the person who cast them.

This book offers an alternative way of thinking, by suggesting more effective ways to protect yourself and avoid being vulnerable. If you want to stop someone from being harmful to you, there are plenty of spells that can help you do so without losing your integrity. We offer a selection in this book. We have also included many spells to help you on a smoother path through life — spells to help in your love life, spells to let you focus your mind on how to gain more friends, and spells to help you get through deadlines at school and at work.

Most of all, we hope *The Girls' Guide to Spells* will inspire you to make up your own spells. Have a good look at the way the spells in this book have been put together, and you will get a feel for how to create spells of your own. The spells that you tailor yourself will often be the most powerful, because you are the only one who can choose and combine exactly the right ingredients for your purposes.

To help you enjoy casting spells, we have included many useful tables and lists of ingredients for spells in this book. All of the items are easy to obtain, and inexpensive too. We have also included many useful tips. These will help you prepare for spell casting, and for what to do after the spell has been cast, while it is doing its work.

We can't show you how to make magical gestures and conjure things up out of thin air, but we can show you how to use spells to help things happen in your life. We hope you make the most of the great potential of spell casting, and let spells help bring the magic back into your life.

What You Need to Know About Spells

ABRACADABRA: SPELLS AND HOW THEY WORK

A spell is like a magical recipe. Put together the right combination of ingredients, and you will be able to make things happen magically in your life.

The ingredients of a spell can consist of almost anything — special thoughts, special words, special objects. These objects do not have to be either expensive or hard to obtain. They can include both things that occur in Nature, such as herbs, semiprecious stones, crystals and essential oils, and things that have been produced artificially, such as candles, colored cords, and even pen and paper. A spell will often incorporate a combination of objects that correspond to your intention with your magic.

It is believed that a form of energy vibrates within the planets, within human beings and animals, and within all material objects, both organic and artificial. It is also believed that we can harness this energy through magical spells.

These vibrations of energy are known as frequencies. Different frequencies have different effects on us in terms of health, emotion and magical intentions. These frequencies, and the things they correspond to, have been observed and noted over the centuries. For example, both rose quartz and the color red have frequencies that relate to love. The most common of the correspondences between energy frequencies and concepts such as love, healing and strength are used in this book.

YOU ARE THE POWER BEHIND THE SPELL

Some spells may not require any ingredient other than yourself. You are the most important part of the spell — you are the one who must work out what you really want. Often a spell will require you to visualize in great detail what you wish, or what you would like to happen. Being able to focus your mind is one of the most powerful tools in spell casting.

But take care when deciding what to visualize. It is often said about magic, "Be careful what you ask for — you might just get it."

Once you have found the right ingredients you will need to raise some energy to empower the spell — usually by dancing, singing or chanting. You can also use the energy of the Earth, by doing a "grounding" exercise (see pages 14–15). The energy you raise within yourself or through the Earth can be directed toward the success of your spell, especially if it is "earthed" in an object used in your spell. This energy will give your spell a great deal of strength. If spells are like cookery, then this energy is like your cooker or stove, transforming the ingredients into something quite unlike their original form. Something magical.

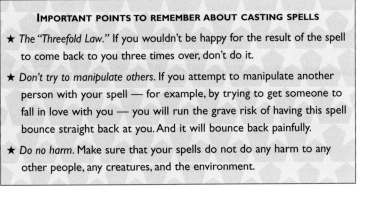

IMPORTANT POINTS TO REMEMBER ABOUT CASTING SPELLS

★ *The "Threefold Law."* If you wouldn't be happy for the result of the spell to come back to you three times over, don't do it.

★ *Don't try to manipulate others.* If you attempt to manipulate another person with your spell — for example, by trying to get someone to fall in love with you — you will run the grave risk of having this spell bounce straight back at you. And it will bounce back painfully.

★ *Do no harm.* Make sure that your spells do not do any harm to any other people, any creatures, and the environment.

Using your intuition

Your intuition — your inner sight or voice, your sixth sense — is a powerful blend of observation, common sense and a clear connection with the wisdom of Mother Nature. There are many theories about how intuition works, and there is much skepticism about its existence. We believe that intuition does exist, and that it can be effective.

When you choose a spell to cast, your intuition will guide you on the right spell to use for your particular purpose. If you are creating your own spell, your intuition will also help you to choose your ingredients and the type of spell to cast. What's more, intuition is very useful for divination purposes — for example, for doing a reading about your life using tarot cards.

One of the most important ways of strengthening your intuition is to believe in it and work on strengthening it. Do so by setting aside some time to sit quietly and "see" or "listen" to your inner thoughts. Your intuition will be stronger when the Moon is either dark or full. At the next Dark Moon, make an "intuition pouch" — see opposite — to help you tune into your deepest thoughts.

A Magic Circle

Before performing a spell, cast a Magic Circle for yourself by visualizing a glow of electric blue flame around you and your spell-working space. This will help focus and contain the energy you raise in your spell.

Making an intuition pouch

YOU WILL NEED:

a piece of dark blue cloth

a dark blue candle

a small bowl

4 drops of one of the following essential oils:
cloves, frankincense, patchouli, sandalwood

a pinch each of 2 of the following herbs:
bay laurel, cinnamon, cloves, mugwort

a length of black string or embroidery thread

Start by cutting out a small circle from the cloth. On a low table, or on a clean cloth on the ground, place a dark blue candle, the bowl containing a mixture of the oil and herbs, the cloth circle and the string or thread.

Light the candle, and turn out the lights. Sit in front of the table or cloth on a cushion, and look into the light. Relax, calm your mind, and focus on the light of the candle. When you feel ready, place a little pile of the herbs on the cloth, saying the following words:

Open the starlit veil of night,
So I may see with inner sight;
By magic's art, reveal to me,
The hidden things I wish to see.

Gather the cloth up with the herbs, and tie up the ends with some black embroidery thread. Wear your pouch at times when you want your intuition to be at its strongest.

MAKING YOUR OWN MAGIC WAND

In spell casting, magic wands are used to help direct energy into a spell object, such as a pouch of protective herbs or a lucky charm.

Magic wands are often made of wood, or of metals such as copper. The simplest way to get or make one is to find a stick that has been thrown to the ground by the wind. Go for a walk through one of your favorite parks, forests or tree-lined streets after a windy day for the specific purpose of finding a suitable branch. Do not be tempted to pull off a branch that is still connected to a tree, because you will cause harm to the tree, and the subtle energy within the branch will be undermined.

Wands were traditionally made from the wood of the rowan tree or the mountain ash. However, this may not be possible for you to obtain. As long as the branch you find fills the following requirements, you can use it as your magical wand. It should be:

★ fairly straight
★ at least 15 inches (38 cm) long
★ about half an inch (12 mm) thick
★ formed from wood that is firm, not diseased, and not too dry

Once you have found the stick that feels right for you, have some fun decorating your wand. With marker pens, draw your favorite symbols, such as stars and the moon, on the stick. You can also cut openings at the ends and then glue a pointed clear quartz crystal at one end and a rounded purple amethyst at the other.

As copper is believed to be an excellent conductor of psychic energy, you could wrap some copper wire (you can get this from a hardware store) over the join between the wood and the rounded stone. Then loop the wire up along the stick to the pointed stone, and wrap it around the join. Use extra wire to attach other objects, such as feathers and beads, to the stick.

Dedication ceremony

When you have finished making your wand, sit quietly with it for a few moments, dedicating its purpose to healing, and to spells that will not harm anyone or anything.

To empower your wand, dedicate it to the four elements. This you can do simply by placing the following on a low table or on a clean cloth on the ground:

your wand

a white candle

your favorite incense stick (with its holder)

a bowl of earth or salt

a bowl of water

a piece of cotton or linen cloth

Light the candle and the incense. Plunge the wand (pointed tip first) into the bowl of earth (*Earth*) and then pass it over the smoke of the incense stick (*Air*). Next, pass it quickly over the candle flame (*Fire*), and dip it into the bowl of water (*Water*). When you have finished, wrap your wand in the cloth, and use it with love and compassion.

Using the Power of Mother Nature

TAPPING INTO NATURE'S ENERGIES

Ever seen a cyclone or a tornado, a volcano or a bushfire, a flood or an earthquake? Imagine being able to harness that sort of energy and use it to improve your life!

Four elements make up the power of Mother Nature — Earth, Air, Fire and Water. In Western and some Eastern philosophies, it is believed that we also have a combination of the four elements within ourselves. Once we have learned to tap into these elements, we can attune ourselves to Mother Nature and increase our own powers. And the energy we gain will make our spells more effective.

The following exercise will help you tap into Mother Nature's power, both within yourself and in the world around you. Start the exercise on a windy day. You will find it an excellent way to feel balanced. You will also find it will make you more confident that you can take control of your life.

Tuning into the elements

AIR: Find a place exposed to the breeze. Stand facing the wind, and feel it blowing against your clothes and skin, lifting your hair. Listen to it, and let the wind stir the energy within you, lifting your spirit and inspiring your mind. Raise your arms to the wind and say:

"I am Air!"

FIRE: Sit comfortably in front of an open fire. Listen to the sounds of the fire as it burns. Feel the heat on your face and body. If you have any music that makes you want to dance, play it now, and dance with the fire, feeling your spirit rising with the flames. As your body heat rises, stop and face the fire, arms wide, and say:

"I am Fire!"

WATER: Sit next to a deep pool, a rippling stream, a waterfall, or the ocean. Imagine swimming into the depths to discover secrets hidden there. Watch the movement of the water and listen to it bubbling and splashing. Put your hands in the water and say:

"I am Water!"

EARTH: Go to a park, a forest or a field where you would feel comfortable about lying down on the ground. Feel the ground beneath you, and smell its scents. Feel yourself sinking into the Earth, enveloped in the arms of the Earth Mother. Feel that your own body is an extension of the Earth, and say:

"I am Earth!"

Take off your shoes and walk barefoot on grass, keeping that feeling of connection with the Earth as you walk.

SPELLS AND THE ELEMENTS

In Western magic, a spell is not properly cast until it has received the energy of the four elements — Earth, Air, Fire and Water.

You can conduct a simple ceremony to anchor the energy of the elements and empower your spell. You will need to use special "tools" to symbolize each of the elements. The table below lists the tools that correspond to each element.

Element	Tool
Earth	Stones, food
Air	Burning incense sticks, bells
Fire	Candles, brass cauldron
Water	Bowl of water, cup of water

It is still believed today, as it was in ancient times, that we can achieve a perfect balance by combining these elements in equal parts. It is believed that doing so can help conjure the power to perform miracles, such as turning non-precious metals into gold or being able to cure any illness. What's more, the balancing of the elements can also add extra energy to a spell.

Once you have finished casting a spell, consider conducting the following little ceremony to harness the energy of the elements.

Harnessing the energy of the elements

Place four "elemental tools" on a small table or a clean cloth. For example, you could gather together a melodious-sounding bell, a red candle, a small glass of water and a bite-size piece of cake or small cookie. Also have a box of matches with you.

Sit comfortably on a cushion in front of your small table or cloth. Relax your body, and calm your mind. Concentrate on your breathing, breathing in to a count of four and breathing out to the same count. When you are ready, do the following four things:

★ Focus on your breathing, feeling that with each breath you are sending the power of *Air* to help your spell succeed. Ring the bell once to link the power to your spell.

★ Focus on the heat in your body, and imagine that you can feel your temperature rising. Visualize the heat traveling through your body, and direct the power of *Fire* into your spell. Once you have imagined this, light a red candle.

★ Focus on the feelings of warm affection and love you have for someone — for example, your parents. Feel the love enveloping your whole body. The element of *Water* corresponds with the emotions, including love. Direct the power of your love into your spell. Once you have imagined this, drink the glass of water.

★ Focus on the ground or floor that you are sitting on. Feel the support and sense the stability. Let these feelings grow within you. Visualize that you are directing these feelings, representing *Earth*, into your spell. Once you have imagined this, eat the food.

When you are ready, extinguish the light of the candle, and sit for a while watching the smoke rise from the wick. Imagine that your spell is going out into the world.

MOON MAGIC

Nature changes its energy in cycles — the cycles of the seasons, the daily cycle of the Sun, and the monthly cycle of the Moon.

If we can tune into these cycles, we can start working with the natural forces, "going with the flow" rather than against it. Let Nature's cycles play an important part in any decision about when to cast a spell.

The different phases of the Moon are said to have a strong influence on magical and natural energies. The cycle begins with the **New Moon**, the one night of the lunar month when the Moon is not very visible in the sky. Spells can be cast during the dark night of the New Moon (sometimes called the **Dark Moon**), or at the first crescent of the New Moon.

As the Moon grows in size and power, she is referred to as the **Waxing Moon**. The most powerful time for casting spells is just before the Moon is completely full. After the Full Moon, as the Moon decreases in size, she is referred to as the **Waning Moon**. Consult the table below for the best types of spells to cast during the different phases of the Moon.

Phase of the Moon	Most favorable for
New Moon (dark night)	Spells for releasing the past, letting go, and finding lost things or hidden secrets
New Moon (first crescent)	Spells for attracting new things into your life, for new beginnings and commitments
Waxing Moon	Spells for increasing, improving and developing things already in your life
Full Moon	Spells for any particularly special purpose
Waning Moon	Spells for protection, for getting rid of bad habits or illness, for reducing or removing negative influences

New Moon spell

On the day before the first New Moon's crescent is due, gather some white flowers, and put the petals in a bowl of water. Take a moonstone or a clear quartz crystal and place it in the bowl of water. When the first crescent appears, take out the moonstone or crystal and hold it up to the Moon. Say the following words:

Gentle face of Maiden Moon,
Before you I do cast this rune;
As to your fullness you shall grow,
So shall this I wish to know:
That [now say what it is you wish]

Put the moonstone or crystal somewhere safe, but show it to the moonlight for the next three nights, repeating your wish (or question), which should be resolved by the time of the Full Moon.

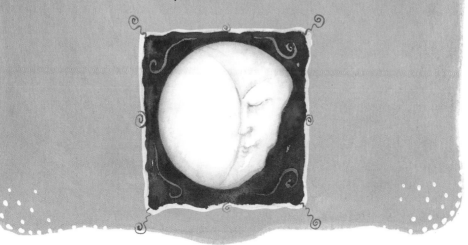

Making Magic Happen in Your Life

CONNECTING WITH THE EARTH

*I*f you feel connected with the Earth, you will find you can link up with the invisible psychic energy that swirls around and within you, the Earth, and the heavens. This feeling will help you raise power for your spells.

Take five minutes to do the Tree of Life exercise — see across. Not only will you feel a deep sense of connection, but you will also feel happier and more focused.

Tree of Life exercise

Sit comfortably on the floor or the ground. Keep your back straight, and your neck relaxed. Take a moment to get rid of the thoughts of the day; allow them to drift away. Let yourself feel relaxed in your sitting position.

When you feel ready, take three deep breaths, close your eyes and imagine that your spine is the trunk of a tree. Now imagine that you have roots reaching down into the Earth from the base of your trunk. Press your feet down on the floor or ground. Imagine that you can feel the cold soil and rock beneath you as you stretch your roots down toward the molten fiery core of our Earth.

Now, with each breath, visualize that you are drawing energy up from the Earth, up through your roots, and up into your spine. Feel the Earth's power flow upward through your body, filling you with energy and nourishment.

While you are feeling the Earth's energy moving through you, imagine that from the top of your head you have branches reaching up toward the sky. Imagine stretching up your topmost branch and reaching toward the sun and the stars. With each breath, draw the energy from the universe down into your body, to join with the rising energy from the Earth. Enjoy for as long as you like the sensation of the energies blending within you, filling you with a sense of joy and peace.

When you are ready to finish this exercise, imagine that you are pulling back your branches from the heavens. With each breath out, send to the Earth any excess energy through your roots.

After finishing the exercise, take a walk in a park, or in a field or forest, to remind you of your connection with the Earth. Try to take a walk through Nature at least once a day.

If you do the Tree of Life exercise in different seasons, you may notice that the energy of the Earth changes in the course of the year. During Spring, the energy is vibrant and new. In Summer, it feels strong and steady. In Autumn, it creates a sense of abundance, and in Winter, the energy feels centered in deep thought and contemplation. See pages 34–35 for more about the seasons and your spells.

YOU CAN MAKE A DIFFERENCE: LEARNING TO FOCUS

Learning to focus is a great way of making your spells work effectively. Focusing skills are required at various stages in the casting of a spell.

FOCUSING ON YOUR INTENTIONS

First, you will need to focus on what you really want from your spell. Begin by imagining that the spell has worked, and you have got what you wanted. Is the result something that you really wished to call into your life? Or did you want something else instead?

If you have trouble deciding what you really want, try collecting a set of images from magazines, books or the Internet, photocopied if necessary. Paste these pictures on a large sheet of paper and hang them in your bedroom, or place them in a journal or specially designed folder with clear plastic "pockets." Also include a recent photograph of yourself.

After a while, a type of "weeding" process will start to happen. Some pictures will not seem quite right. Feel free to continue working on your stash of pictures, adding and removing images. This is a powerful way of focusing on what you want.

FOCUSING ON SUCCESS

Focus is also required for visualizing the success of your spells. The key to visualization is to imagine things in detail. See your friend feeling better after a long sickness, or see yourself meeting a nice person on a date. Spend some time imagining how this would feel. Use all your senses — for example, imagine that you can smell the perfume or cologne of your new friend, or hear your sick friend talking with a strong, firm voice.

You will also need to focus on raising energy within yourself. Doing the visualization exercise on pages 20–21 is an excellent way to achieve this. It will enable you to concentrate on imagining that energy is stirring within you. Once you can feel this stirring, you will be able to play with directing the energy to various areas of your body. Focus on directing the energy toward your hands, imagining that the energy is collecting and pulsing into your fingertips. Your hands are one of your most important tools for spell casting.

Improving your focusing skills

Here is a simple exercise for improving your focusing and visualization skills. Take one of the pictures you have collected, and study it for a good five minutes. After this period, or once you feel that you know the picture thoroughly, tear it in half. Place half of the picture face down so that you cannot see it, and look at the other half. See if you can complete the picture in your mind's eye. Practice this by using other images as well, and gradually lessening the time spent on familiarizing yourself with them.

FINDING YOUR MAGICAL NAME

Names can be very important. What we are called may have a powerful effect — it may hurt us, or empower us. To help you bring out and connect with your "magical self," find a magical name that represents to you your own unique energy. This name can come from an ancient myth or legend or a fictional character in a book or movie, or can even be something that you invented or that just "came" to you in a dream or vision.

If you can't decide on a name, conduct the following little ceremony at Full Moon. Keep your magical name to yourself. Share it only with others whom you can trust totally.

Finding your magical name

YOU WILL NEED:

a big silver or white bowl, filled with water

a white candle, matches

your intuition pouch (if you have made one — see pages 10–11)

Sit where you can see the light of the Full Moon. Better yet, see if you can capture the image of the Moon in the water.

Take a couple of deep breaths, and ask the Moon to help you find your magical name. Light the candle, and let the melted wax pool on top of the candle. Then pour the wax into the water. Look at the pattern formed in the water by the cooled wax. Does it form a symbol, or a letter of the alphabet? Let your mind go blank, and continue looking at the pattern. The first name that pops into your head will be your magical name.

FINDING AN ANIMAL HELPER

In many cultures, each person has a "totem" — an animal or bird with which they have a special relationship, in both the physical and spirit worlds. Finding our animal totems or helpers can help us connect with the natural world around us, as well as giving us insights into ourselves and others. Sometimes animals can give us warnings that things aren't right about another person, or that a natural disaster is imminent.

Spell for finding your animal helper

YOU WILL NEED:

a few dabs of patchouli oil

a handful of catnip herb (fresh or dried)

At the time of the New Moon, dab some of the oil on your wrists and your feet, take the catnip, and go to a place where you can see the Moon — outside, or at a window. Sprinkle the catnip on the ground around you or on the windowsill, saying:

In spirit form or flesh, I summon thee,
In love and trust, my wild and totem kin;
Thy untamed and ancient wisdom share with me,
And may friendship, never ending, now begin.

LIAM CYFRIN

Take note of your dreams or your thoughts for the next three days and nights after casting this spell. You may find yourself suddenly thinking of a particular animal, or you may see one on a documentary or in a book and feel an affinity with it. You may also find that you experience an unusual sighting of an animal on your walks or near your home, or have an unusual encounter with a particular animal, or that a certain animal appears frequently.

25

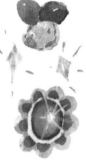

FINDING AND USING A PENDULUM FRIEND

A pendulum consists of a stone or metal weight tied to the end of a piece of string or a length of chain. It can be a very helpful tool for finding answers to many questions. Most New Age stores stock pendulums. However, you can easily make one for yourself. You will need to find a smallish, tear-shaped stone (such as an amethyst, a quartz crystal or a faceted piece of lead crystal) with a point at the bottom.

The stone must be heavy enough to keep some tension along the line by which the pendulum will be held. A hardwood pendulum, or even one shaped from modeling clay, may also be used. It is important that the pendulum swings freely from its string or chain.

After you've found or made your pendulum, spend some time just sitting and holding it, linking it with your personal energy. You can even name it if you like, but be sure to ask it if it likes the name you have given it!

USING YOUR PENDULUM

When you are ready, hold the pendulum in your right hand if you are right-handed, or in your left hand if you are left-handed. Rest your elbow firmly on a stable surface. Hold the string between your thumb and forefinger.

First ask the pendulum which way is "yes." This will differ for each pendulum and the person using it. Your "yes" may swing back and forth, sideways, in a circle clockwise, or counterclockwise. Then ask it which way is "no," and take note of the direction it moves.

At first the pendulum may be a little slow to respond, so you will need to be patient. Try holding the string at different points along its length. The more you use the pendulum and develop a personal connection with it, the more responsive it will become. You can hold it over a piece of paper with a question written on it, and read the question out loud.

You can also hold it over a map, and ask where to find something you've lost, or where to find love. To ask questions about someone you know, write the person's name on a piece of paper and hold the pendulum over the name, or over a photograph of that person, a lock of their hair or their personal belongings.

You can ask your pendulum just about anything, as long as your questions expect the answer "yes" or "no." When you have finished, thank the pendulum for its help, and wrap it in a special cotton or linen cloth or bag for safekeeping.

STONE SPIRITS

It is sometimes believed that each crystal, gem or stone has its own special spirit. Before using a stone or crystal for your spells, hold it, and ask its spirit stone to lend its powers to your spell, for the good of all, and harming none.

YOUR SPECIAL SPACE: IDEAS FOR DECORATING YOUR ROOM

Over the centuries, it has been found that bringing something that represents Nature into your home will help you feel a little more connected to the energy of the Earth. Being able to see how vast the Earth's power is will help us put some of our problems in perspective.

Consider decorating your room as a cavern of wonder and delight — a haven where you can escape from the troubles and pressures of the everyday world. Look into using as many pictures and fabrics that remind you of the natural world as you can, to allow you to link into its wonder and its power.

Use as much natural fabric as possible in your decorations. If you are into crafts, make your own pictures, covers for your bed and small boxes or ornaments. This will remind you how clever you are with your hands. Having objects and pictures that you have made yourself in your haven will make it powerful, and in it you will be able to regenerate your strength.

To remind yourself of the natural world, set up a small table in your bedroom or special room. Place on it some candles, incense, your favorite stones and gems, and small pictures of your favorite people.

Keep the following on this little table, or in a special box:
- ★ your intuition pouch (see pages 10–11)
- ★ your magic wand (see pages 12–13)
- ★ your pendulum (see pages 26-27)
- ★ your spell diary (see pages 36-37)
- ★ any candles, stones, herbs, incense and essential oils that you like using in your spells

Be careful not to let your room become too cluttered. It is believed by a number of ancient civilizations that clutter slows down the energy circulating around your space. Keep your room tidy, and air the room regularly. Also keep your dressing table drawers tidy, and make sure there is no accumulation of rubbish under your bed. If you keep your room clear of clutter, you will experience a corresponding effect in your life, and your ability to focus will be improved.

CLEARING YOUR SPACE AFTER AN ARGUMENT

To protect your space, cast an imaginary circle of blue light right around the room. Do this when you are feeling vulnerable or upset. Always make sure that you cut a doorway in the light as you walk into and out of your room.

If you have had a really unsettling argument with someone in your room, burn some incense or a calming essential oil, such as lavender, to clear the air of any negative energy left over from the argument. Also ring a melodious bell in each corner of your room, to further clear the air.

Spells and You

PUTTING YOUR OWN SPELLS TOGETHER
STEP-BY-STEP

Making up your own spells isn't difficult. Just follow the steps below.

Step 1: Imagine what you are wishing for

Take some time to imagine how it would be to have your wish come true. Imagine in as much detail as you can how you would feel when your spell worked. See the money for a new car, hear the waves on a beach as you relax on your longed-for holiday, or smell the aftershave or perfume of your new love. Also imagine the full consequences of the spell. Make sure that your spell will cause no harm to any person or creature, or to the environment.

Step 2: Imagine that you can make a difference

Visualize that your will can make a difference in the world. Don't be defeated by any feelings that you don't deserve what you want. If you feel your confidence is undermined, ask your friends for help.

Step 3: Choose the type of spell

There are many different types of spells to choose from. Your spell may be activated by repeating a phrase, by lighting a candle, by putting together stones, herbs, essential oils and other ingredients, or by combining some or all of these actions. For inspiration, look at the spells in this book.

Step 4: Gather your ingredients

At this stage, you should feel that you know what you want your spell to do. You should also feel that you have the power to make your wish come true.

Empowered with these feelings, gather your ingredients. Choose those that you know to have the right vibrations for powering your spell — or those that you *feel* to be right.

Step 5: Find a special place
For your spell-making space, use your bedroom, a special space in your home, or anywhere else you feel safe and comfortable and won't be interrupted.

Step 6: Tap into your energy and link it with the Earth's
In your special space, and with your ingredients around you, do the Tree of Life visualization (see pages 20–21), to tap into both your own energy and that of the Earth. When you have tapped into this form of energy, you will be able to power your spell.

Step 7: Cast your spell
When you feel a sense of power coming over you, say your words or do the actions of the spell within your special space. To add extra power to your spell, cast it on the appropriate day (see pages 32–33), and during the appropriate phase of the Moon (see pages 18–19) and the appropriate season (see pages 34–35). Above all, cast your spell with good intentions.

Step 8: Let the spell go
Once you have finished your spell, allow the energy that you have sent out with the spell to return within you. Take a piece of rock and hold it, to help you feel grounded again.

Step 9: Watch out for new opportunities
Over the next few days, look out for any coincidences or unusual occurrences. These are often indications that your spell has started to work. If you are presented with an unexpected opportunity, take it — and see where it leads you.

CHOOSING THE RIGHT DAY

You may find it effective enough to rely on your intuition when choosing the right day for your spell. However, there are also some traditional correspondences between days and types of spells that you may find helpful. Use the table below to work out which day corresponds to the particular type of spell you want to cast.

Day of the week	Suitable spell type
Sunday	Spell to gain insight
Monday	Spell to understand your dreams
Tuesday	Spell to protect yourself from enemies
Wednesday	Spell to help you pass exams
Thursday	Spell to acquire money
Friday	Spell to attract love or friendship
Saturday	Spell to protect your home or business

Another way you can work out when to cast your spell is by finding out what zodiac sign the Moon is in each day. Each sign has its own energy that you can tap into in order to power your spell along. As the Moon passes through each sign in turn, its energy is affected by the qualities of that sign.

The table below lists the different energies that are generated by the Moon while it is in a particular zodiac sign.

This relationship between the Moon and the zodiac sign is not related to the *phases* of the Moon (Full Moon, New Moon etc.), but to the *part of the sky* the Moon is in.

Finding out which sign the Moon is in at a given time is easy enough. There are many astrological or "Moon" calendars or diaries available, as well as guides on the internet.

Position of Moon	Type of energy	Type of spell suitable
Moon in Aries	Increased vigor, new projects, independence, protection when you have been involved in an argument, desire, competition	Spell to protect yourself from being drained in an argument
Moon in Taurus	Prosperity, security, affection, artistic and musical talents, resources, nature, quality	Spell to open up our creativity
Moon in Gemini	Adaptability, intelligence, communication, transportation, choices, learning	Spell to help you with your studies
Moon in Cancer	Home and family, the past, intuition, safety and protection, healing and nurturing	Spell to let go of a painful past
Moon in Leo	Children, creativity, courage, strength, vitality, romance, recognition, leadership	Spell to attract popularity
Moon in Virgo	Organization, health, perfection, gardening, pets, attention to detail, attaining skills in a desired field	Spell to help you finish your school or college assignments
Moon in Libra	Love, attraction, justice, balance, beauty, decoration, socializing, partnerships	Spell to attract a new love or friend
Moon in Scorpio	Secrets, intuition, emotions, passion, intensity, psychic skills, endings and beginnings	Spell to help you end a relationship
Moon in Sagittarius	Travel, study, confidence, optimism, success, good fortune, adventure	Spell to help you study
Moon in Capricorn	Responsibility, achievement, structure, authority, commitment, wisdom, reputation	Spell to help you commit to a relationship
Moon in Aquarius	Originality, freedom, new ideas, friends, new groups of friends or new organizations, being unconventional	Spell to help you stand up for yourself
Moon in Pisces	Spirituality, imagination, psychic abilities, dreams, compassion, healing, escape	Spell to help a friend

CHOOSING THE BEST SEASON

The energy of each season can also have a tremendous effect on your spell. Find out the best season for your type of spell, and then try some of the following.

SPRING SPELLS

Spring is the best season for spells to attract new love or money, and spells to cleanse or heal.

AUTUMN SPELLS

During Autumn, cast spells for giving thanks for your achievements, sharing your prosperity with others, investing money, and getting rid of bad habits or addictions.

SUMMER SPELLS

Summer is the best season for spells for personal power and success, strengthening relationships and friendships, beauty, and protection.

WINTER SPELLS

During Winter, do spells to help you sort out your life, spells for inner personal development and for aiding your studies, and candle magic.

A spring cleansing-and-new-growth spell

Take a crystal to a fresh stream or the ocean, and swish the crystal in the water.
Say the following words:

Gone are troubles, pain and strife,

Cleansing waters bring new life.

Imagine that the water is washing away all stresses and worries from the past, renewing your energy, and bringing you a fresh start. When you remove your hand from the water, wrap your crystal in a cloth. Take it home, and put it beside your bed, so that you can hold it first thing on a spring morning to encourage new growth in your life.

Spell to strengthen energy and see fairy folk

On Midsummer's Eve (the Summer solstice), mix up some elderberries and mugwort herb in a bowl, and take the bowl outside to a place where you feel safe. Sprinkle the herbs around you in a circle, and sit inside the circle quietly, allowing yourself to feel part of the Earth and the plants. Take note of the small movements of the plants, and the subtle vibration of energies around you.

To strengthen the feeling of these energies around you, imagine that they are like little garden fairies who are weaving a web of safety and protection around you. To call up the "little folk," say the following:

Fairy folk of this fair place, Come and show me your sweet face;
A friend am I, to do no harm, I call to Thee with magic charm.

An autumn-leaf banishing spell

Pick a large fallen leaf that is soft enough to write on without breaking. With a suitable pen, write on the leaf anything you wish to let go of — for example, fear or poverty. Light a small bonfire of autumn leaves. Throw your leaf on top of the pile and say the following:

Burn and be finished, burn and be done; Fading now with the waning Sun.

Watch the leaves burn. See the smoke rise, and imagine that your troubles are being harmlessly released and dispersed into the air.

Spell to strengthen your hopes and dreams

On the night of the Winter solstice, take a white candle and carve on it symbols or words representing your hopes and dreams for the coming year. Rub some pine or juniper oil onto the candle, and place it where it can safely burn down throughout the night.

Now light the candle. Focus on it, seeing your hopes and dreams taking shape in your life.
Say the following:

I light this candle in the dark of night, A symbol of that inner Light,

That brings my hopes and dreams of worth, Together with the Sun's rebirth.

STARTING YOUR OWN SPELL DIARY

Consider starting a journal to record the spells you have cast or are interested in casting. Keeping a record will give you new insight into your spells.

Make a spell diary or journal that is uniquely your own. It can be anything from a prettily covered exercise book to a special blank journal with a lock and key. You can decorate the pages with photographs of yourself, family and friends, and magazine pictures of your favorite things and places.

Make the diary as colorful and as decorative as you want. Consider hand-making your own spell diary, or purchasing a journal made from handmade paper, with leaves or petals embedded in the paper.

Decorate the cover of your spell diary with your favorite pictures, or carefully glue on glass "gems," feathers and beads. To keep your spell diary protected, use a plain white feather or a black and white one as a bookmark, or draw the rune 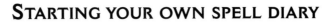 for protection called "algiz."

MAGIC BOOKS OF SPELLS

Be sure that you only choose spells that are ethical and will do no one any harm. If you have seen a spell in someone's private journal of spells (in some magical traditions, these private journals are called "Books of Shadows"), always make sure to ask permission before copying the spell for your own use.

Take care also with your choice of spell. In earlier times, there were textbooks on sorcery and magic, called "grimoires." They contained practical advice for a huge range of spells. Unfortunately, a number of grimoires contained spells that were designed to be manipulative, and called down ancient, erratically-tempered spirits. People who cast spells from these books often found that the spells attracted a great deal of unbalanced energy. This energy sometimes led to bad accidents, and even death.

A RECORD OF YOUR SPELLS

Your diary should be your private journal of spell work. Put in as many details of your spells as you can remember. List the ingredients, when you did the spells, and how you did them. Note in your diary how you raised the energy for your spell. Also comment on whether you felt you were able to direct enough energy into the spell.

Apart from keeping all your spells in one place, your spell diary can also be a useful place for noting any interesting or unusual events that occur after you have cast your spell. Use the diary as well to jot down any dreams you may experience the night after you have cast a spell. Also write down your interpretations of your dreams, and see if this provides any insights.

Keep your journal in your special space, or beside your bed. If your friends are keeping spell diaries as well, always make sure you ask permission before copying anything out of their diaries.

Using Candles in Spells

CHOOSING AND PREPARING THE RIGHT CANDLE

Candles are some of the simplest tools of spellcraft. They can be used for virtually any type of spell. Wax has traditionally been used for magic because of its ability to absorb magical intention.

The color of the candle is usually chosen according to the purpose of the spell. See the table below for some traditional associations between the spell's purpose and candle colors. However, if the colors recommended in the table do not feel right for you, use a plain beeswax candle instead. You could also meditate quietly to discover what color would best suit your purpose.

Also consider the shape of the candle. Again, use your intuition to decide what would suit your spell. You could perhaps choose a round candle for spells seeking comfort, happiness or peace, or an upright candle for spells seeking a new love, a new direction in your life or an increase in your fortunes.

SYMBOLS FOR CANDLES USED IN SPELLS

To help bring the energies of the elements — Air, Fire, Water and Earth — into a spell, you can draw or carve the symbols of these elements onto your candle, wand or other magical tool.

Air △   **Fire** △

Water ▽   **Earth** ▽

Depending on the purpose of your candle magic spell, you could also carve other symbols along the side of the candle. For example, for a money magic spell you could carve a dragon, or the magic symbol for Jupiter.

Jupiter ♃

CANDLE PREPARATION

Whatever spell you are casting, you will first need to prepare the candle. Wax can pick up negative energy quite easily, so it may be a good idea to wash the candle lightly with salted water. Then dry it thoroughly and, if you have time, wrap it up in a cloth of the same color as the candle, and leave it in the light of the moon.

When you are ready to use the candle in your spell, shake a few drops of aromatherapy or massage oil onto your fingers and smear over the candle. Oils, like colors, should ideally correspond with the purpose of your spell. The table gives examples of oils that correspond with particular magical purposes.

Purpose of spell	Corresponding color	Corresponding oil
Love	Red	Patchouli
Friendship	Pink	Mugwort
Courage	Orange	Endive
Money	Green	Cinnamon
Confidence	Yellow/gold	Basil
Peace	Blue	Camomile
Power	Purple	Frankincense

A candle spell for attracting good fortune

Spells concerning finances and fortunes should be performed on a Thursday (see pages 32–33). In magic, Thursday is linked with Jupiter, because this planet's energies are traditionally associated with money issues.

In terms of the signs of the Zodiac, Jupiter corresponds with Sagittarius, so one of the best times to perform this spell would be between November 24 and December 21. If this time of year is too far away for you, do the spell on a Thursday during the period when the Moon is waxing (see pages 18–19).

YOU WILL NEED:
a small bowl
a strong, sharp needle
a green candle
a candle holder
a gold-colored coin

Into your bowl, measure out two teaspoons of sweet almond or vegetable oil, and add the following essential oils (if available):
1 drop ginger
3 drops lemon balm (*Melissa*)
5 drops patchouli

With your needle, carve a four-leaf clover on the candle, and then spread the oil mixture over the candle. Place the candle in its holder, and slip the gold coin under the candle holder. Light the candle, and imagine that good fortune is becoming a reality for you. Leave the candle in a safe place, allowing it to burn itself out.

A candle spell for feeling good about yourself

When you are feeling negative about yourself, try the following candle spell to reaffirm your true strength and beauty.

YOU WILL NEED:
a very special sheet of paper
your favorite pen
essential oil /perfume of your choice
a yellow candle
a suitable candle holder

On the piece of paper, write down all the things you like about yourself. This may seem hard at first, but you can make things easier by imagining that you have an "inner friend" who really likes you and is pointing out your good qualities, or is defending you against negative thoughts from your conscious mind. List all the positive qualities you know you have. For example: "I am a careful thinker," "I am a loyal friend,"or even:
"I have cute toes."

Spread your favorite essential oil or perfume over the yellow candle while reading out loud, and with confidence, all of the qualities you have written down. Place the candle in the candle holder, and fold the piece of paper so that it will fit under the holder. Light the candle and allow it to burn to the end. The smoke of the candle flame will send out to the universe all your positive thoughts about yourself.

Keep the piece of paper in a safe place, and take it out whenever you feel down. It will remind you of your inner strength and power.

Spells at Home

DOING SPELLS FOR FRIENDS AND FAMILY

You can do many types of spells for your friends and family, including healing and protection spells. Often you will find that casting a spell for another person requires some insight into that person. When you cast spells for a friend or family member, review what you know about that person, and discuss the spell with him or her.

Before you cast a spell for someone other than yourself, get permission from the person whom the spell will benefit. In fact, it is always a good policy to wait until you are asked before casting a spell for someone else — unless you are dealing with an emergency. Have a chat with the intended recipient of your spell to find out what he or she really wants. As you would do with spells for yourself, form a specific objective in your mind.

You can adapt many of the spells in this book so they can be cast for someone else. Use the same instructions, but also include in the spell's ingredients something connected with your friend or family member, such as a lock of hair. This will indicate that the spell should be directed to someone other than yourself.

Take care when choosing someone else as the recipient of a spell. This sort of magic will strengthen the bond between you. *Never* use skills in this way to manipulate others, or to get them to do something they would not normally wish to do. Also make sure that you can trust the recipient of your spell not to try to manipulate *you*. The bond you forge with a spell for someone else is a two-way street!

You can also help family and friends by casting a spell to send them a healing or protective energy. This energy will be a mix of your own power and that of the Earth.

Spell to send energy to another

As with all spell casting, do this spell in a place where you will not be disturbed.

Start by generating some energy within yourself. How you do this is your own choice — you may like to chant, or perhaps dance to your favorite music. The idea is to raise the energy until you feel your body temperature rising. At this point, stop what you are doing, and visualize the energy swirling inside of you.

Stand or sit on the ground, and visualize the Earth's energy being attracted to your own energy. Feel a line of energy moving up through the soles of your feet and then up through your spine to the top of your head. Stretch your arms up, and feel the energy also moving up to your hands.

Next, visualize that this energy has the particular quality you wish to send to the other person — for example, the ability to help a broken leg to heal. When you are ready, pick up the item belonging to your friend or family member, and imagine that all the energy you have built up and tapped into is now flowing into the object. Hold the object until you sense that you should stop. Remember to keep grounded with the Earth's energy (see pages 14–15) so that you do not inadvertently drain yourself.

This spell is very powerful. It will send directly to your friend or family member whatever it is you wish for that person. Place the person's object in a safe place until you next see him or her. Then advise the other person to have the object safely nearby whenever the energy is needed.

FINDING NEW FRIENDS

There will be times in your life when you feel you don't have a friend in the world. Always remember: just as energies ebb and flow with the movement of the seasons, this time is only a phase. Also, the feeling of being without friends can provide invaluable — although sometimes painful — learning experiences.

Do not be afraid to keep learning more about yourself, and about how to behave with friends. Remember that one of the keys to attracting new friends is the ability to respect both yourself and others. Try also to remember that you are a very powerful person, and that, even if you have negative feelings about yourself, you are capable of making changes.

If you are feeling less than confident, try the candle spell on page 41 to help you feel good about yourself and perceive your positive traits rather than focusing on your bad ones. You can also try the following attraction spell. It includes a visualization that will help you move on from the state of feeling powerless and unable to find friends who like you for who you are.

If you use the attraction spell, you may find that when you feel happier and stronger within yourself, others will become attracted to you. However, as with any spell, don't then just sit back and wait for things to happen on their own. Be sure that you open the door to friendship in other ways. Don't be afraid to be the first to say hello to someone.

Attraction spell

two strands each of yellow, green and gold embroidery cotton

all six strands should be 36 inches (1 m) long

Tie the strands together at one end, and attach the tied end to something stable, such as the knob of your bedroom door. Position a chair in front of the door, and sit down facing the door.

Focus on relaxing your body and your mind. When you are ready, imagine that the energy of the Earth is moving up into your body through your feet and the chair legs. Visualize the energy as a golden light, shining within you. Feel the light burning away any negative thoughts and feelings that you have stored up about your past friendships.

Bask in this light, and imagine that it is attracting the attention of people who are able to see the special person you really are. Visualize the light growing, spreading down your arms and into your hands. Start to braid or weave the threads together, weaving the golden light into the threads as you do so. As you are weaving, chant the following words:

Heart of gold and soul divine,
Bright my inner star does shine;
Come, my friends, I call to you,
Come share the joys of friendship true.

When you are ready, let the braided thread hang from the door as a symbol that, whenever you walk out of the door of your bedroom, you are walking into a new reality where you have friends worth having.

You could also braid the threads into a bracelet and wear it, particularly when you are feeling lonely or depressed. When you are feeling low, imagine the golden light flowing from the bracelet and dissolving any feelings of negativity you have.

FRIENDS IN MAGIC: THINGS TO DO TOGETHER

There are a number of fun things you can do with a friend or a group of friends to strengthen your spell-casting skills, and tap into the energy flow of the Earth, the Moon and the cosmos.

As much spellcraft is based on the observation of the cycles of Nature and the seasons, consider meeting your friends every Full Moon for a special night. During your Full Moon meetings, just have fun together, swapping special spell ingredients that you have either made or grown. Wear moonstones, and have each member of your group bring a white drink or food, such as round biscuits powdered with white icing sugar. Be creative, and make special wish boxes for each other, or friendship bracelets of silver and white threads, beads and feathers.

Use this time for discussing different spells, and suggesting variations that may make a spell more effective. As the Full Moon is a time of heightened psychic energies, also consider using this time for practicing your divination skills — tarot, I-Ching and so on — on each other. If any of your group needs a bit more energy for healing, for protection or for a spell to encourage a better flow of money, use the Full Moon gathering to practice doing a spell together for the benefit of one of your members.

Spell for calming arguments

In even the closest friendship or the most tightly knit group, arguments can flare up.
Try this spell to resolve your differences.

YOU WILL NEED:

a silver bowl of water that two people can hold together easily

a small bowl of salt

a stick of sandalwood incense

a mauve, light blue or pink candle

You and your friend should sit opposite but close to each other, with the bowl
of water and other items between you.

Now each of you should put a pinch of salt into the bowl in turn, saying:
By the powers of Earth, we are united.

In turn, too, blow some incense smoke over the bowl, saying:
By the powers of Air, we are connected.

Take turns to pass the bowl over the candle, saying:
By the powers of Fire is our [anger/pain/hurt/fear] transformed.

Now hold the bowl up together, saying:
By the powers of Water is our friendship cleansed.

As you hold the bowl together, think of the recent argument, misunderstanding or
hurt, and remember the negative feelings you experienced. Visualize these feelings as a
murky substance flowing out through your arms and hands and into the bowl.
When you are both ready, take the bowl and empty it together either in a
running stream or down the drain in the bathroom.

SPELLS FOR A HARMONIOUS HOME LIFE

Family dynamics can sometimes be improved if one person stops adding to the sense of disharmony. Even if you feel that other members are not doing the same, cultivate an atmosphere of closeness and integrity within your family.

If your family life is anything but harmonious, try to exercise good will and respect to help resolve the situation of disagreement or unhappiness. Try to follow these three golden rules:

* ★ Give unconditionally and happily.
* ★ Understand and balance the needs of yourself and your family.
* ★ Keep true to yourself.

Keeping true to yourself may be difficult in a situation of disharmony. But it is here that you can call into play the skills you have learned in this book. Empower yourself by linking with the forces of Nature (see pages 14–15) so that you can feel strong, and effect changes. It often takes just an injection of positive energy to turn a negative situation around. Plant or keep in your home something that will encourage peace and harmony. The herb lemon balm, often grown in home gardens, is sometimes called the "Happy Herb." Keep a bowl of fresh crushed lemon balm leaves on a table or mantelpiece in your home.

Learning to avoid distractions will help you focus on what you hope to achieve rather than on the negative situation. To help develop your concentration or focusing skills, sit in a room with two or more demanding noises being made at once (such as a stereo, television and alarm clock). Focus on one noise at a time, and try not to let the others distract your focus.

Spell to attract harmony into your home

You will need to gather as many of the following herbs as you can. You will only need a small amount of each (half a teaspoon if the herb is dried, or 5 leaves if it is fresh):

Basil	**Betony**
Cumin seed	**Mistletoe**
Rosemary	**St John's Wort (hypericum)**
Star Anise	**Valerian**

YOU WILL ALSO NEED:

some rose petals/rose essential oil

some geranium flowers/geranium essential oil

a small glass mixing bowl

a light blue drawstring bag

**a small piece of rose quartz/clear quartz crystal/any other small stone
that makes you feel calm and happy**

Mix the herbs and flowers (or oil) in the bowl, and pour the mixture into the bag. Also place in the bag the stone you have chosen.

Sit for a minute and imagine you are a tree, sending your roots into the Earth and your branches toward the stars (see pages 20–21). Bring the Earth's and the stars' energy into you, then send it out through your hands onto the herbs, and say the following words:

By the powers of these Herbs, the Earth and the Stars,
Happiness and harmony shall abound.

Draw the strings of the bag together, and tie a knot to keep the contents within the bag. Place the bag over or near the front door, at the entrance to your bedroom or in a room where it is most needed.

Spells for Success

STARTING A NEW SCHOOL OR JOB

The first day at a new school, or in a new job can be harrowing. Try this spell to help you gain confidence for the big day.

Spell for confidence

The night before you start school or your new job, gather the following:

a mirror

2 red candles

a piece of paper/lightweight cardboard that is easy to fold

a pin

The mirror should preferably be full length. If you don't have a full-length mirror, find the largest mirror you can safely carry into your bedroom or the safe space where you are doing this spell.

Place the candles on either side of the mirror, ensuring they are reflected in the mirror. Light the candles, and switch off the lights in the room. Stand in front of the mirror and look into the reflection of your eyes. Without moving your focus away from your eyes, say your name, and then say something positive about yourself — for example, "My name is Antonia Beattie, I have a nice smile," or "My name is Amargi Wolf, I am warm and friendly." Think of as many positive things as you can, and say them after saying your name.

When you are ready, drip some wax from each candle onto the middle of the paper. Let it set a bit, and then use the pin to scratch your name into the wax. Fold the paper over the wax. Take it with you on your first day safely tucked into your pocket, or carry it in your school bag or briefcase in a small padded bag. If you feel the need for some more support, also tuck into the small bag or your pocket a picture of a person or animal representing courage and inner strength to you.

CONFIDENCE FROM YOUR TOTEM ANIMAL

Also consider taking an image of your totem animal (see pages 24–25). Draw a quick picture of it, or find a picture in a magazine. On the morning of your first day, include your totem animal picture in your pocket or bag. Now you can imagine that you have your totem animal standing beside you, ready to walk (or fly) with you throughout the day.

If you do not have a totem animal, but would like to have the feeling of an animal present beside you, sit in a quiet space for a few moments and let your mind go blank. Think of an animal that symbolizes fearlessness. The first image to come into your head will be your helper animal for the day.

A SPECIAL STUDY SPELL

According to a number of Western magic traditions and many Eastern cultures, the mind can be trained to expand and to grow, and is like a muscle that needs to be exercised constantly.

As you may have guessed by now, a lot of spells are based on the use of the power of your mind to think in a more focused way. This power will focus the spell, which will then be powered by both your own energy and the energy drawn from the Earth.

The following study spell to "stretch" time falls within the group of spells that can help you change your mindset. We often fail to realize how much time we take up *not* focusing on the task at hand. When we are trying to study to a deadline, like an exam, we may feel a bit unfocused about the job because of a particular fear. This fear is usually about the future, a future in which we will have to sit through that exam or deliver that report or term paper. All of a sudden, doing anything else — even washing dirty dishes — will seem preferable to studying.

Spell for stretching time

ALLOW AT LEAST TEN MINUTES FOR THIS SPELL. YOU WILL NEED:

a white candle, matches

a candle holder

a clock showing the right time, preferably with a second hand

Light the candle, and place the clock so that you cannot see the time on it. Sit quietly, watching the flame flicker and glow. This will help you anchor yourself in the present. If you are feeling slightly panicky, also focus on your breathing — you may be hyperventilating. To alleviate the feeling of panic, focus on breathing in to a count of four and breathing out to a count of four while you look at the candle's flame.

When you feel ready, close your eyes. You will see an image of the candle flame. Imagine moving that image so that it is positioned over your "third eye" — a point over the middle of your forehead. This will help you anchor yourself to the present.

Now turn the clock so that you can see the time. Watch the second hand as it moves around the clock face for a full minute. Sense that this hand is moving at a slow and measured pace. Feel everything starting to slow down. Breathe to a count of four seconds in, four seconds out.

Imagine that your whole day is filled with more time than you know what to do with. Extinguish the candle, put the clock back into its place, and carry this feeling of stretched time back to your work.

Keep with you the feeling of time stretching out. Remember throughout the day to enjoy each moment of your time.

PASSING EXAMS

Feelings of panic or inadequacy can prevent you from accessing all the information you need for passing exams. There are a number of spells that can help you overcome this, but be aware that they can never substitute for actual studying. Although spells cannot do the studying for you, they are a wonderful way of helping you achieve your full potential.

MUSIC TO HELP YOU STUDY

To help with study, especially if your subject is a language or grammar, or if you are learning how to use word skills, consider listening to some classical music. For especially effective music, try the works of Johann Sebastian Bach or Wolfgang Amadeus Mozart (in particular, Mozart's Sonata for Two Pianos in D Major, K 448).

To help release stress while studying, listen to musical chants, either modern new-age recordings or those based on ancient Gregorian chants. The rhythms of deep breathing in the chants will remind you to breathe deeply, and will aid you in controlling any feelings of panic.

Spell to help pass exams

YOU WILL NEED:

a small muslin bag or a bag made of any other natural fabric

a fluorite stone (if this is unavailable, use a clear quartz crystal instead)

YOU WILL ALSO NEED THE FOLLOWING MIXTURE OF ESSENTIAL OILS:

3 drops basil

3 drops cinnamon

3 drops clove

20 drops rosemary

20 drops lemon balm

Substitute fresh or dried herbs if you do not have or cannot find any of these oils.

Before your exams, on a Wednesday sometime during the period of the waxing Moon, rub the oils (or herbs) onto the stone, directing your mind toward being clear and aware, calm and confident. Also direct your memory toward being retentive and sharp.

Put the stone (and herbs, if any) into the bag, and keep it on the desk before you as you study.

On the night before your exams, recharge the stone with some fresh oils or herbs, and light a pale blue candle. Place the stone in its muslin bag in front of the candle and focus on the light, calming your thoughts and releasing the tensions in your body.

When you are calm, imagine that you are sitting in the exam room and smiling.

Visualize being able to answer every question, and enjoying the feeling of being able to communicate what you know about the topic of the exam. Revel in this feeling for a few moments.

Take the stone out of the bag, and pass it over the flame of the candle. This will embed your thoughts of success in the vibrations of the stone. Wrap it up in a piece of natural cloth, and take it with you into the exam.

MAKING A POWERFUL GOOD LUCK CHARM

A charm was traditionally a magical phrase that could be repeated to help bring luck and protection. Lucky charms today, however, are any objects that have favorable associations, such as a favorite ring or stone.

Over the centuries a number of different shapes and certain natural objects, such as herbs, crystals and gems, have come to be thought of as lucky. These objects include birthstones — stones that have a special link with particular signs of the zodiac. Use the table below to find out the birthstone for your particular sun sign. Check the table on page 78 if you do not know which constellation corresponds with your birth date.

Sun sign	Corresponding birthstones
Aries	Bloodstone, opal, diamond
Taurus	Amethyst, moss agate, sapphire
Gemini	Lapis lazuli, moonstone, emerald
Cancer	Cornelian, pearl, ruby
Leo	Amber, black onyx, peridot
Virgo	Jade, sardonyx, jasper
Libra	Chrysolite, coral, tourmaline
Scorpio	Malachite, topaz, aquamarine
Sagittarius	Turquoise, moonstone, topaz
Capricorn	Jet, garnet, ruby
Aquarius	Jade, amethyst, sapphire
Pisces	Opal, pearl, moonstone

Spell for a lucky charm

an orange, violet or green drawstring bag

seven green candles

a yellow feather (not from a dead bird — find someone who has a pet canary)

a dried chili bean

a cowry shell

your birthstone

a hazelnut

a pinch of one of the following herbs — golden seal, angelica, yellow mustard seeds, St John's Wort (hypericum) or nutmeg

Put the bag and the spell's ingredients in front of you, with the seven candles placed in a semicircle around and behind them. You can also burn some incense while casting this spell.

Light the candles and pick up the bag. Put the ingredients into the bag in the following order, while saying these words:

(feather)	*By the power of Air,*
(chili bean)	*By the power of Fire,*
(cowry shell)	*By the power of Water,*
(birthstone)	*By the power of Earth,*
(hazelnut)	*By the power of Spirit,*
(herb)	*By all the powers of Nature.*

Once the ingredients are in the bag, hold it tightly and say:

And the power of my True Will.

Close the bag and say, finally:

My life shall be blessed with good luck.

The bag will now be charged with objects symbolizing the elements, the spirit, Nature, and your own true energy. Carry it with you wherever you go.

Spells for Protecting Yourself

GIVING YOURSELF PERMISSION TO FEEL STRONG

There are many different types of protection spells. Special amulets, talismans and charms, made in ancient times, are still made today as protection against specific dangers.

Protection spells can act as a defence against a wide range of problems, from loss of health (disease) or loss of money, status or your job, to faithlessness in a partner, betrayal by a friend or deceit in business dealings.

The protection spells described in this section have been developed to combat common fears. Note that spells can enhance your ability to deal with your fears, but must never be used as a "crutch." They must only be used to improve your chances of fulfilling your true potential, or to give you some "breathing space" while you work out what you want to do. If you are walking into a situation that is unavoidable and also dangerous, either physically or emotionally, a spell can help you to keep on your toes and pass safely through the experience.

If you have an inherent belief that you will be victimized, there is a very good chance that you will be. Consider changing your mindset. Remember that you are a strong individual, even if you haven't yet given yourself the opportunity to develop your strengths.

One of the most effective ways of giving yourself the space to discover these strengths and to protect yourself is to create a magical sanctuary. This sanctuary can be created within your mind to help stop other people's negative energy affecting you and getting you down.

Creating an internal magical sanctuary

Sit comfortably, and relax. Connect with the energy of the Earth. Try the Tree of Life visualization on pages 20–21, imagining that you are a tree with roots buried deep within the soil of the Earth and your branches brushing against the stars in the sky.

When you are fully relaxed, visualize your private sanctuary. It may be a cottage nestled within the roots or branches of your tree, or anything from a cave to a castle, a forest grove to an island. Create strong images in your mind, with as much detail as possible. Let your imagination go — in your "Inner World," nothing is impossible.

Whenever you feel emotionally frail or vulnerable, you need only take a moment to go to your special sanctuary for healing and inner strength. You may like to add a clear pool of healing waters, or a special tree that has magical healing fruit you can eat for strength and courage. You can also use this place to communicate with your higher self, your guardian angel or your totem animal.

AN INVISIBILITY SPELL

Our minds are very powerful instruments, and the most important ingredient in most spells. They help us to visualize and to focus our magical intentions.

Humans have been fascinated for centuries by invisibility spells and spells for being in two places at the same time (bi-location). There are some traditional spells that ask you to put together a range of ingredients to make up a substance that will make you effectively invisible. While actual invisibility is quite impossible, we can use our minds and the vibrations of certain natural objects to send out signals to other people around us that we are not present. Being screened from attention in this way is a far more workable alternative than true invisibility.

Spell for making "invisibility powder"

Grind together some dried heliotrope flowers or leaves, and some fern spores. Fern spores can be acquired by putting a sheet of paper under a fern for a few days.

Grinding these plants will produce a powder, which you should sprinkle over yourself, or put in a little sachet with a sardonyx stone. Wear this sachet around your neck, or carry it with you. Ferns and sardonyx are renowned for their ability to make the person carrying them seem to disappear, and this is most useful if there is anything you need to do without attracting much attention.

Here is a useful spell to use if you are feeling uncomfortable around a group of strange people. Again, as with any spell, use your intuition to avoid finding yourself in any dangerous situation.

Visualization for protection

If you are caught without your invisibility powder or sardonyx and are experiencing unwanted attention, imagine that you are surrounded by a bright blue light. Keep the image of this light close to you, like an aura around your whole body.

You can do this visualization anywhere, and without needing to take your attention away from the problematic person. You can also move around freely within your blue cocoon. The blue light is a form of vibration that creates a type of psychic haze through which people find it difficult to focus on you.

A sign that the blue cocoon image is working is if the other person's eyes appear to glaze over, or if the person's conversation starts becoming less focused.

Always remember to ground the blue protective light into the Earth once you do not need it, by imagining that the protective shield is melting away through you, down your feet and into the ground. If you forget to do this, you may become a bit concerned when your friends don't seem to want to talk to you!

DEALING WITH DIFFICULT TEACHERS AND FRIENDS

A difficult person is someone who does not communicate truly with others. We all go through phases of being difficult in this way. Sometimes our feelings of anger, frustration and insecurity may be so overwhelming that we just cannot communicate cleanly and respectfully.

The best form of protection from your own as well as others' negative energies is to have a strong inner center — to feel strong within yourself. When dealing with a difficult person, you may find it helpful if you can feel confident and happy in the knowledge that you are okay. Then you won't get caught up in the other person's "psychic sludge," even if it seems to be directed straight at you.

If you feel angry, frustrated or insecure yourself, do the visualization spell on pages 20–21 to help you feel grounded. This spell will also help you gain perspective, and some insight into your feelings.

Another useful way of handling another person's negative energies is to treat them with unfailing generosity or goodwill. This will help you avoid being hooked into the bad energy generated around the other person. This energy can be very contagious, and can create an unhealthy dynamic between you and the other person.

THOUGHTFULNESS IS AS GOOD AS A SPELL

If you normally have good relations with a friend, yet this friend is being very difficult at the moment, make an effort to do something thoughtful. You could give your friend chocolates or flowers, for instance. A thoughtful act is as good as any spell to help a friend pull through a difficult phase.

If you are dealing with a difficult teacher or boss, visualize an outward-facing mirror between you and the other person. Then everything the person directs at you will get bounced straight back at him or her!

Green is a very healing color for troubled communication. Carry a piece of green obsidian with you to the classroom or workplace whenever you are likely to meet a difficult person, or wear a ruby to attract a bit more kindness from the people around you. The color red vibrates with the energy of love.

If you have been hurt by someone's pettiness, cruelty or thoughtlessness, again do the visualization exercise on pages 20–21, imagining that the person's words are caught in your branches. Visualize these words turning into autumn leaves that turn from yellow to orange and then finally to red. See the leaves falling from your branches onto the ground and decomposing quickly, to be reabsorbed by the ground and turned into fertilizer!

FOCUSING ON YOUR BREATH

To help develop your focusing skills, sit comfortably. Feel your breath as it goes in and out of your nose. As you discover your thoughts starting to wander, gently bring your awareness back to feeling your breath. You will find that this becomes easier with practice.

COPING BETTER WITHOUT CURSES

Spells can help you in most situations. The spells in this book are designed to help you have a full, exciting life, unfettered by unreasonable fears or feelings of helplessness or of being a victim. Use them with a good heart, and have fun with them.

Never allow a sense of superiority or arrogance to cloud your judgment about what type of spell to cast. Always remember that you should respect not only yourself, but also the people, creatures and environment around you.

We have often mentioned in this guide the principle of doing a spell only when it harms none. Please honor this wholeheartedly. Never, even for a practical joke, jab pins or other pointed objects into an image of a person or creature. If you wish to protect yourself from a genuinely destructive person, make a powerful "mojo bag" to help protect you from negative behavior.

A mojo bag for protection

TO MAKE A MOJO BAG, YOU WILL NEED:

some soft, thin leather

a pen or marker

black embroidery thread or a thin black leather thong

5 of the following herbs:

Agrimony	Clove
Anise	Rue
Bay laurel	Verbena
Cinnamon	St John's Wort (hypericum)

5 drops essential oil — frankincense, amber or clary sage

To make the bag, cut a circle out of the leather and make or punch an even number of holes around the circumference.

In the center of the circle, draw a five-pointed star, and pull the thread or thong through the holes.

Place in the middle of the circle five pinches each of five of the herbs. On top of the herbs, sprinkle five drops of essential oil. Carefully gather up the edges of the circle, and tighten the thread. Tie the thread together once so that you safely capture all the ingredients in the mojo bag, and then pull the thread twice more around the top before tying it securely. While you do so, chant the following words, raising as much energy and willpower as you can:

Herbs of power, magic charm,
Protected I am from all harm.

Make sure that the thread or leather thong is long enough for you to tie the ends with, and hang the mojo bag around your neck. Carry it with you whenever you feel you need some extra protection. The warmth of your body will release the scent of the herbs and the essential oil. When you are not wearing your mojo bag, keep it stored in a safe place in your bedroom or other special place.

Spells for Your Love Life

STONE CASTING TO FIND OUT IF SOMEONE LOVES YOU

*S*emiprecious stones can pick up subtle vibrations around you, and can help you work out whether or not someone likes you. Semiprecious stones come in many colors and many types, including quartz crystals, moonstones, amethysts, and other beautiful stones. They may be polished, or left in the rough. In your spell diary (see pages 36–37), note all the stones you have, adding to the list as you add to your collection. Find out each stone's magical qualities, and use your intuition to tailor the information to your own circumstances. For example, as there are many different types of love in your life, choose different stones that you feel resonate with these emotions — one stone may vibrate to feelings of passionate love, while another may correspond to the love you have for your mother.

You can also find a specific stone to represent magically the *person* you like. At your favorite stone supplier, pick the first stone you touch or see while thinking of the person. Do the same for all your favorite people, and note which stone represents which person.

Also gather some stones that indicate *feelings* to you. The stone's finish can point to an emotional state. One in the raw state may signify that a person loves you but doesn't know it yet. A stone polished into a smooth pebble, not yet finished shape, may mean that the person loves you but is not ready to express this emotion. If the stone is in a heart shape, this may be an indication that the person loves you and is ready to connect with you. Use your intuition to work out what each stone means to you.

The *color* of the stone is also an indication of the type of love that a person may have for you. White usually symbolizes a platonic friendship, pink a harmonious friendship, and red a strong attraction. A clear quartz crystal, this could mean that the person has no special feelings for you.

Doing stone castings

Spell 1

To do a simple stone casting, gather together the stones representing your favorite people. Mix them in a cloth bag. Hold the bag in your hands, and ask to see the person who will be your next love. Throw the stones out of the bag, and take note of the stone that lands nearest to you. This stone represents your next love.

Spell 2

Another simple stone casting will help you discover whether a particular person loves you. Gather together the stones that represent certain emotions to you, as well as the clear quartz crystal. Mix them in a bag, and hold the bag while you ask to see what a particular person feels for you. Put your hand in the bag and pull out one stone only. This stone will indicate whether your friend loves you — yet!

GATHERING STONES

If you love the look and the feel of stones, consider keeping your collection of stones, as well as any new stones you get, in a box lined with natural fabric, such as cotton, silk, flax or hemp. Before storing your new stones, cleanse them with salty or running water to remove any negative vibrations.

A CLARITY SPELL TO ENSURE YOU CHOOSE RIGHT

Sometimes we may be strongly attracted to someone who seems very charismatic, good-looking, exciting or simply just "cool." However, once the fixation dies down, we may sometimes discover that this person would not have been right for us, and we would have ended up in a disappointing or unhappy relationship.

It's hard to see clearly when we are totally besotted with someone — "hit by Cupid's arrow." So, before you work on getting involved with a particular person, you need to be clear on what your needs within a relationship really are. Then you can decide whether a specific person can help you fulfill your needs.

Clarity spell

Do this clarity spell if you want help to avoid choosing the wrong person with whom to have a new relationship.

Write down on a piece of paper what you want in a relationship, starting with the really important things — for example, good communication, affection, friendship, fun, mutual respect, support, caring and sharing.

THEN GATHER THE FOLLOWING INGREDIENTS:

2 pinches dried basil leaves

2 pinches dried rosemary

2 pinches dried marjoram

2 pinches cinnamon powder

2 geranium flower petals /2 drops geranium essential oil

a small clear quartz crystal

a small drawstring bag of blue fabric

Perform this spell outside, or next to a window where you can see the sun.

At midday, place the two geranium petals on the middle of the piece of paper you've written on, and then sprinkle the herbs on top of the petals. If you're using geranium essential oil, pour the herbs first, then sprinkle the two drops of oil over the herbs. Hold the crystal between the paper and the sun, so that the sunlight shines through it onto the herbs. Imagine that you are thinking clearly, and are aware of the realities of your situation. Say firmly, three times:

O mighty Sun, at your greatest height
All is shown in your clearest light.
By my spell help me to see
If he [she] is really right for me.

Fold the herbs and flower into the paper, and place the package in the little bag together with the crystal. Carry the bag in your pocket or around your neck for as long as you feel in need of clarification about your feelings for a particular person.

This spell will also help attract the right person to you — someone who shares your priorities in a relationship. While you are searching for a new person, you can add to your list of relationship priorities, and recharge the spell as often as you like. Do so by adding a few more herbs and drops of essential oil to the original piece of paper while saying the words three times.

GETTING RID OF YOUR JEALOUSY

Jealousy is a very uncomfortable emotion, which often stems from the feeling that you are powerless to change your own life. Never allow this emotion to take hold of you. Remember that you are powerful, and can make important changes in your own life.

We are often placed in competition with each other at school, college or work, and this may cause us to have negative feelings about ourselves. Often we will compare ourselves with another person we perceive as more successful or lucky, without knowing what sacrifices and strains have led to the other person's experience of good fortune.

Like the seasons, we all have ups and downs in the flow of energy in our lives. At times we experience Summer's energy of success and popularity, and at others we feel Winter's introspective energy. It is rare that two people experience the same ebbs and flows at the same time, and so it's pointless to compare your own life with someone else's. We all have our individual destinies and challenges to face.

If you don't feel powerful, focus on what you want, and your connection with the Earth. Once you have tapped into the Earth's energy (see pages 14–15), you will feel you can do anything you want.

Also try the following anti-jealousy spell, to relieve your feelings of jealousy or hurt in a relationship.

Spell to counter jealousy

GATHER 5 PINCHES OF 3 OF THE FOLLOWING DRIED HERBS:
ST JOHN'S WORT (HYPERICUM)
BORAGE
LEMON BALM
BASIL
GERANIUM

Focus on your feelings of jealousy and hurt while grinding your chosen herbs. Use a mortar and pestle, or rub two rocks together. If you are using rocks for grinding the herbs, choose ones that do not crumble easily. Grind your emotions into the herbs, imagining your feelings running down your arm and into the bowl.

When you are ready, put the ground herbs into a bowl with a cover. Take the covered bowl to a private outdoor area, preferably on a windy day.

Holding the bowl in your hands, take a moment to face the breeze, and feel it blowing against you. Imagine that the flow of air is linked with your energy, and that the pressure of the air is raising the energy within you. As your energy rises, lift the bowl in your hands and say:

To the Wind that does blow, my jealousy I throw;
With the Wind it does flee, from envy I am free!

Now remove the cover from the herbs and cast them into the wind so that they blow away from you, taking with them your jealousy and hurt.

Again feel the air swirling around you. You will notice that you feel lighter and more energized after doing this spell.

PREPARING YOUR ENERGIES FOR THAT BIG DATE

As you prepare for an important date, consider enhancing your attractiveness not only by your choice of clothes and make-up, but also by releasing your energy and letting your inner beauty glow brightly.

You can do this by doing the following meditation, based on your chakras, the seven energy centers running through your body. This meditation is also useful for getting rid of pre-date jitters, and will help you feel strong and balanced throughout your date, giving you poise and a sense of confidence.

Meditation for energy release and confidence

Sit on the floor or the ground in a quiet place. Use a soft cushion if the surface is too hard. Imagine that energy is flowing from the Earth through to the base of your spine, and "lighting up" your spine in the form of a red glow. Continue to imagine the energy flowing up your spine through each chakra. The colors of the chakra energy centers correspond with the seven colors of the rainbow. Feel each area being "lit" up with its appropriate color (see the table across).

Once the energy reaches the top of your head, allow it to flow back to the ground. Imagine that the energy is looping back up your spine, feeding your body with a continuous flow of vitality and strength. Keep this feeling with you when you go on your date. When you get back home, imagine reversing the flow of the energy into the ground, and allow the light in the chakras to dim.

Position of chakra in your body	Corresponding color
Base of spine	Red
Sacrum (just below the navel)	Orange
Solar plexus	Yellow
Heart	Green
Throat	Blue
Middle of the forehead (the "Third Eye")	Violet
Top of the head	Purple

SEEING YOUR AURA

An aura is another form of energy generated by the vibrations in our bodies. To see your aura, sit or stand in front of a mirror with a dark or white background behind you. Half close your eyes and "look" at the energy field around your head. Can you make out a haze of color around your head — your aura? If you can, see whether the haze is either close to your head or flaring out.

The aura in this area of your body is called a nimbus. Often, when we are nervous, the nimbus is close to our heads, or quite dark. To help with any feelings of nervousness before a date, imagine a purple haze of energy flaring all around your head, giving you a sense of calm. Try this while standing or sitting in front of the mirror.

ATTRACTING A NEW LOVE INTO YOUR LIFE

Spells often work by using ingredients that match their purpose. For example, we may use everyday objects such as magnets to signify attraction, or chewing gum to show that the spell will "stick"!

Try this magnet spell to attract new love or friendship into your life.

Special magnet spell for attracting new love

YOU WILL NEED THE FOLLOWING INGREDIENTS:

a piece of lodestone/a small magnet

an even number of rose petals

a small feather (preferably pink; if not possible, choose any pretty color — don't use black!)

a small shell (preferably a clam shell, conch or oyster shell)

a small red cloth bag

2 drops jasmine or ylang ylang essential oil

piece of heart-shaped paper, red (craft paper is fine)

36-inch (1-m) length of pink or red embroidery thread or string

a pen

Put the lodestone or magnet, rose petals, feather and shell into the cloth bag. Sprinkle the essential oil over the ingredients. Put the bag to one side.

On your piece of paper, write all the different qualities you would like your future love to have. Take your time over this step, and think about what you really want in the person — a good sense of humor? A caring and respectful attitude? List each quality on the piece of paper by initial only, so that you can fit all the qualities you want. As you write down each initial, say the word out loud.

Fold the paper up fairly small, and tie one end of the embroidery thread securely around it. Sit at a table or on the floor, with the paper the full length of the thread away from you, and the loose end of the thread close to your hand.
Place the bag in front of you.

Hold the end of the thread and slowly drag the paper to you, imagining your new love being drawn into your life. Say the following words:

I draw my true love unto me,
By power of Earth and Sky and Sea,
By Free Will and harming none,
You hear my call and soon will come.

Now draw the folded paper heart into your bag, and use the end of the thread to tie up the bag. You can carry the bag with you until your new love appears, or use the excess thread to hang the bag from your neck. However you choose to carry the bag, do not cut the thread.

FINDING YOUR TRUE LOVE

There are many traditional spells for discovering your true love — and many not-so-traditional ones for the same purpose. Some inspire dreams in which you see your true love, some give you the initial or the spelling of your love's name, and some predict that the first person you see after doing the spell will be your true love.

Follow tradition, and cast your true love spell at the sighting of the first New Moon after Midsummer's Eve. Midsummer's Eve is an important time for casting spells. The energy of the Summer solstice is useful for spells relating to all types of relationships— with family, friends and lovers. The New Moon is the best time to help all new ventures get off the ground. Try the following spell.

PURIFICATION BATH

Before you do any spells, have a quick "purification bath" to help clear any negative energy collected throughout the day, and put you in a different frame of mind. As you are washing, imagine all negativity, stress or anxiety being washed from your mind and emotions as well as your body.

True love spell

Do this spell during the first New Moon after Midsummer's Eve. Write the following verse on a piece of white paper, or in your spell diary (see pages 36–37):

All hail, new Moon, all hail to Thee!
I prithee, good Moon, reveal to me
This night who shall my true love be;
Who he is and what he wears,
And what he does all months and years.

You will then need to go outside and prop yourself against a fence post or, traditionally, a stile (if you can find one). Look up at the new crescent, and take out your piece of paper or diary and recite with a firm voice the verse you have written down. If you are good at memorization, it would be ideal if you could say the words from memory instead.

When you have done this, go inside and place your piece of paper or diary next to your bed.

Before you go to sleep that night you can also do one of two things: sprinkling two drops each of pine and patchouli essential oil on a handkerchief and placing it under your pillow, or burning an incense stick of elderflower or orris root.

Be aware of your dreams that night and upon waking in the morning write a list of all the people you remember seeing in your dream, whether by name (if you know them) or by description (if you don't). The person who features most prominently in your dream, perhaps through doing something nice for you, will be your true love.

ARE YOU COMPATIBLE?

It has long been thought that the position of the planets at the moment we are born affects many aspects of our lives, including our personalities. Astrology deals with the influence of the planets, the sun and our moon, and studying this, it is believed, can give us great insight into people's characters. Astrological readings can be far more complex than just knowing the position of the sun when a person was born, but sun sign astrology can still provide a useful indication of what a person is like, and whether that person is compatible with you.

The chart below is a list of compatible sun signs. The left-hand column lists the birth dates for the particular astrological sun signs. For example, if you were born between July 23 and August 23, your sun sign is Leo. Look at the right-hand column to see who is compatible with you as a lover.

However, this chart is a rough guide only. There are a number of reasons why a person "clicks" with another person, although you may find you have friends and loves who all have birthdays around the same month.

Your sun sign	Date	Compatible lovers
Aries	March 20 to April 20	Leo, Sagittarius
Taurus	April 21 to May 21	Virgo, Capricorn
Gemini	May 22 to June 22	Libra, Aquarius
Cancer	June 23 to July 22	Scorpio, Pisces
Leo	July 23 to August 23	Aries, Sagittarius
Virgo	August 24 to September 23	Taurus, Capricorn
Libra	September 24 to October 23	Gemini, Aquarius
Scorpio	October 24 to November 23	Cancer, Pisces
Sagittarius	November 24 to December 21	Aries, Leo
Capricorn	December 22 to January 20	Taurus, Virgo
Aquarius	January 21 to February 18	Gemini, Libra
Pisces	February 19 to March 19	Cancer, Scorpio

GLOSSARY

amulet	a small object that has magical, protective powers
astrology	the study of how the movements of the sun, moon and heavenly bodies correspond with various aspects of our lives
aura	a glowing, colored energy field that emanates from all living things
chakra	a line of energy running through a number of energy centers situated in the middle of our bodies. In the most widely used system, there are seven chakras, starting from the base of the spine and ending at the top of the head
Dark Moon	the night before the New Moon
divination	seeking the future and understanding the past
grimoire	a book that is a compilation of spells, magical techniques and magical mysteries that have been used over a period of time
grounding	connecting the body's energy with that of the Earth
I-Ching	(also known as the *Book of Changes*) an ancient Chinese form of divination
Midsummer's Eve	(also known as the **Summer solstice**) the longest day of the year
mojo bag	a bag that holds the ingredients of a spell
mortar and pestle	a mortar is a stone, marble or ceramic bowl against which herbs, salt and other ingredients may be ground into a powder by the pestle, a rounded, stone-tipped utensil
nimbus	the **aura** or halo around the head
psychic energy	a form of energy that can be felt when focusing on the spiritual qualities within yourself, and the energy of the Earth and her creations, such as the rocks, plants and animals
rune	magical symbols first used in Ancient Nordic and Germanic cultures; can be used for **divination**, and are inscribed on talismans and amulets
solstice	the time when the sun is at its furthest point from the equator — the **Winter solstice** and the **Summer solstice**
Summer solstice	see **Midsummer's Eve**
stile	set of steps in a wall or a fence so people can get over, but animals are prevented from doing so
sun signs	in **astrology**, the signs of the zodiac that indicate the position of the sun in the heavens when you were born
talisman	a stone or other small object that has been given a special magical purpose
tarot cards	a deck of 78 cards, divided into the Major Arcana of 22 cards and the Minor Arcana of 56 cards, the cards representing certain aspects of life; tarot reading is a very popular form of **divination**
Winter solstice	the shortest day (and longest night) of the year

This edition published by Barnes & Noble, Inc.,
by arrangement with Lansdowne Publishing

2001 Barnes & Noble Books

M 10 9 8 7 6 5 4 3 2 1

ISBN 0-7607-2494-6

Published by Lansdowne Publishing Pty Ltd
Sydney NSW 2000, Australia

Commissioned by Deborah Nixon
Text: Antonia Beattie, Amargi Wolf
Illustrator: Penny Lovelock
Designer: Robyn Latimer
Editor: Avril Janks
Production Manager: Sally Stokes
Project Co-ordinator: Alexandra Nahlous

Set in Cantoria MT on QuarkXPress
Printed in Singapore by Tien Wah Press (Pte) Ltd